Countries of the World

Switzerland

by Mike Graf

Consultant:
Annina Luck
Cultural Section
The Embassy of Switzerland

Bridgestone Books
an imprint of Capstone Press
Mankato, Minnesota

Bridgestone Books are published by Capstone Press
151 Good Counsel Drive, P.O. Box 669, Mankato, Minnesota 56002
http://www.capstone-press.com

Library of Congress Cataloging-in-Publication Data
Graf, Mike.
    Switzerland/by Mike Graf.
    p. cm.—(Countries of the world)
    Includes bibliographical references (p. 24) and index.
    Summary: Describes the landscape, culture, food, animals, sports, and holidays of
Switzerland.
    ISBN 0-7368-1109-5
    1. Switzerland—Juvenile literature. [1. Switzerland.] I. Title. II. Countries of the world
(Mankato, MN.)
DQ17 .G73 2002
949.4—dc21

2001003230

Editorial Credits
Blake Hoena, editor; Karen Risch, product planning editor; Linda Clavel, designer; Erin Scott,
    SARIN Creative, illustrator; Alta Schaffer, photo researcher

Photo Credits
Audrius Tomonis-www.banknotes.com, 5 (bottom)
Blaine Harrington III, 8, 14, 16
Chip & Rosa Maria Peterson, 6
Dave G. Houser/Houser Stock, 10
Flag Folio, 5 (top)
TRIP/Mountain Sport, 18; A Tovy, 20
Unicorn Stock Photos/Steve Bourgeois, 12
Joe Viesti/The Viesti Collection, Inc., cover

1 2 3 4 5 6 07 06 05 04 03 02

Table of Contents

Fast Facts

Name: Switzerland or Swiss Confederation
Capital: Bern
Population: More than 7 million
Languages: German, French, Italian, and Romansh
Religions: Roman Catholic and Protestant

Size: 15,942 square miles (41,290 square kilometers)
Switzerland is about twice the size of the U.S. state of New Jersey.
Crops: Grains, fruits, and vegetables

Maps

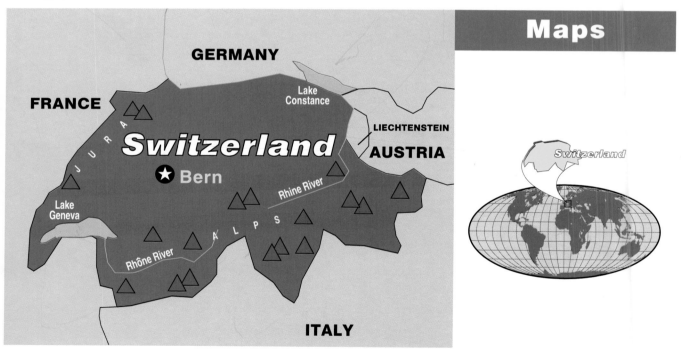

Flag

Switzerland's flag has a white cross on a red background. The arms of the cross are equal in length. The flag was first used by the canton of Schwyz during the 1200s. Soldiers flew the flag before and during battles. In 1848, the flag became the official flag of Switzerland.

Currency

Switzerland's unit of currency is the Swiss franc. There are 100 rappen (or centimes) in a Swiss franc.

In the early 2000s, about 1.75 Swiss francs equaled 1 U.S. dollar. About 1.2 Swiss francs equaled 1 Canadian dollar.

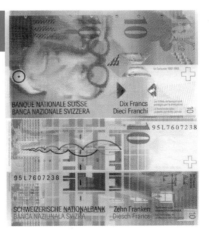

The Land

Switzerland is in central Europe. It is one of Europe's smallest countries.

Switzerland is surrounded by five other countries. Germany is to the north. France borders Switzerland to the west. Austria and Liechtenstein are to the east. Italy is to Switzerland's south.

Switzerland is a landlocked country. It does not border on any oceans or seas. But Switzerland has many lakes and rivers. The Rhine and Rhône Rivers begin in Switzerland. Lake Geneva and Lake Constance are the largest lakes in Switzerland.

Most of Switzerland is mountainous. The Alps are in southeastern Switzerland. The Alps cover more than half of the country. The Jura Mountains are in northwestern Switzerland.

The Central Plateau lies between the Alps and the Jura Mountains. This area also is called the Mittelland. The Mittelland has many lakes, hills, and valleys. Most Swiss live in this area.

Most Swiss live in the Mittelland.

The Alps

The Alps are the largest group of mountains in Europe. They stretch across Switzerland, Germany, Austria, Italy, and France.

In winter, snow covers the Alps. Avalanches and landslides are common. Snow and earth may suddenly move down a mountainside. The Alps also have glaciers. These slow-moving sheets of ice create caves in the mountains. Switzerland has more than 3,000 caves.

In summer, the glaciers melt. Water from the glaciers creates many waterfalls. The water flows into Switzerland's rivers and lakes.

The Alps have many tall mountain peaks. Dufourspitze of Monte Rosa is the highest peak in Switzerland. It is 15,203 feet (4,634 meters) above sea level. The Matterhorn is another tall peak. It rises 14,692 feet (4,478 meters) above sea level. In the mid-1800s, this mountain became famous for the many people who died trying to climb it.

The Matterhorn is a famous mountain peak.

Life at Home

Most Swiss live in the Mittelland. This area has many cities and small towns.

Because of Switzerland's small size, people in rural areas usually do not live far from a city. Switzerland's small size also makes land expensive. Few people can afford to own homes. People in cities often live in apartments.

In rural areas, people may live in traditional style homes. These houses include stone farmhouses and chalets. Chalets are A-shaped. This shape allows snow to slide off the roof of the houses.

Almost everyone in Switzerland knows how to read and write in several languages. Switzerland's four national languages appear on Swiss francs.

The Swiss often help people from other countries. The Red Cross was established in Switzerland. The Red Cross helps prisoners of war. It also helps people affected by natural disasters such as floods or hurricanes.

Many Swiss live in apartment buildings.

Going to School

Children in Switzerland start school at age 6 or 7. They must attend school for at least nine years.

Swiss schools are divided into two parts. Primary school is similar to first through fifth grades in North America. Students learn to read and write in primary school. They also study math, art, and music.

Students then attend secondary school for two to three years. Secondary school prepares students to learn a trade or to continue their education.

After secondary school, most students receive vocational training. They may take classes to learn a trade. They also may find an apprenticeship. Apprentices receive on-the-job training in a trade such as baking or plumbing.

About 25 percent of students go to an advanced secondary school. Advanced secondary schools prepare students who want to attend a university.

Swiss children begin school at age 6 or 7.

Food

Switzerland is famous for chocolate, cheese, and pastries. In 1875, the Swiss invented milk chocolate. The world's three largest chocolate factories are in Switzerland.

In Switzerland, swiss cheese is called Emmentaler. This cheese is aged until holes form in it. Gruyere and Appenzell also are popular cheeses.

The Swiss make several types of pastries. Basler Leckerli is like gingerbread. Birnbot is a bread with dried fruits in it.

Potatoes are common in the Swiss diet. The Swiss usually boil or roast potatoes. They use potatoes in meat stews. Raclette is a popular Swiss dish of melted cheese over boiled potatoes.

Fondues are traditional in Switzerland. Cheese is melted in a pot. People then dip bread into the cheese.

Switzerland is famous for its pastries.

Animals

The animals in Switzerland are similar to those found in most of central Europe. Roe deer, ibex, and chamois live in the Alps. Ibex are wild goats. Chamois are a type of antelope that can climb steep mountain slopes.

Many other animals live in Switzerland. These animals include badgers, lynx, foxes, otters, and beavers.

The Swiss protect many of their wild animals. In 1909, Switzerland's government created the Swiss National Park in southeastern Switzerland. This park protects wildlife in the Alps. People are not allowed to hunt or to build in the park.

Bears no longer live in the wild in Switzerland. But many people come to see the bears of Bern. These bears are kept in a round, open pit in the city of Bern. It is a tradition for couples to feed the bears on their wedding day.

Ibex are a type of goat that live in the Alps.

17

Sports and Recreation

The Swiss enjoy winter sports. People downhill and cross-country ski. Switzerland has many ski resorts in the mountains. The Swiss also enjoy bobsledding, tobogganing, ice skating, and curling. To play this game, people slide objects called stones across the ice toward a target.

The Swiss play many other sports. They play soccer, volleyball, and basketball. Tennis also is popular. Martina Hingis is a famous tennis player from Switzerland.

The Swiss enjoy many other activities. They often walk or bike. They hike in the mountains. At night, they may go to the theater or to concerts.

Yodeling is a traditional type of singing in Switzerland. Long ago, mountain hikers discovered that they could hear each other across great distances if they yodeled.

Mountain hiking is popular in Switzerland.

Holidays and Celebrations

Swiss families often gather to celebrate Christmas. Traditionally, the celebration begins with the arrival of the "Christkind" or the "petit Jésus" on Christmas Eve. This child is dressed as an angel and represents Jesus Christ. Young children are told that the Christkind brings gifts. On Christmas Eve, people decorate and light their Christmas trees. Parents then give presents to their children.

Swiss National Day is August 1st. On this day in 1291, the first three Swiss cantons came together as one country. Cantons are similar to states and provinces. The Swiss celebrate Swiss National Day with fireworks, concerts, and yodeling.

The Swiss have several festivals throughout the year. Some festivals are related to the fall harvest. Others celebrate the popular foods of certain regions. Wine and cheese festivals are common. The Swiss also hold many music festivals during the summer.

People often wear traditional clothes at festivals.

Hands On: Make Dumplings

Knopfli or spaetzli (dumplings) are a popular type of food in Switzerland. Have an adult help you with the stove.

What You Need

10 1/2 ounces (298 grams) flour
4 medium size eggs
1/4 cup (50 mL) water
1 1/4 teaspoons (6 mL) salt

large bowl with cover
large pot
slotted spoon
grated cheese (optional)

What You Do

1. Mix flour, eggs, water, and 1 teaspoon (5 mL) of salt together in a large bowl. Blend the dough until it is smooth. Cover the bowl and leave out for 30 minutes.
2. Fill a large pot with water, add 1/4 teaspoon (1 mL) of salt, and bring the water to a boil.
3. Add small pieces of the dough one at a time to the boiling water. Remove the dumplings with a slotted spoon when they float to the water's surface. Repeat for the rest of the dough.
4. Arrange the dumplings on a dish. Sprinkle them with grated cheese or eat them plain.

Learn to Speak German

German, French, Italian, and Romansh are Switzerland's national languages. But German is the most commonly spoken language. Around two-thirds of Switzerland's population can speak German.

hello (good day)	Guten Tag	(GOOT-en TAHG)
good-bye	auf Wiedersehen	(OWF VEE-der-zay-en)
How are you?	Wie geht es dir?	(VEE GAYT ESS DEER?)
please	bitte	(BIT-tuh)
thank you	danke	(DAHN-kuh)

Words to Know

avalanche (AV-uh-lanch)—a large mass of ice and snow that suddenly moves down a mountainside

canton (KAN-tohn)—a region of Switzerland; cantons are similar to states and provinces in North America.

glacier (GLAY-shur)—a slow-moving sheet of ice found in mountains and polar regions

landlocked (LAND-lokt)—not bordered by oceans or seas

landslide (LAND-slide)—a large mass of earth that suddenly moves down a mountain or hill

yodel (YOH-duhl)—to sing in a voice that changes rapidly between high and low sounds

Read More

Netzley, Patricia D. *Switzerland.* Modern Nations of the World. San Diego: Lucent Books, 2001.

Rogers, Lura. *Switzerland.* Enchantment of the World. New York: Children's Press, 2001.

Useful Addresses and Internet Sites

Embassy of Switzerland
2900 Cathedral Avenue NW
Washington, DC 20008

Embassy of the United States, Bern
Jubiläumsstrasse 93
3001 Bern
Switzerland

CIA—World Factbook—Switzerland
http://www.odci.gov/cia/publications/factbook/geos/sz.html
Swiss Embassy—Welcome Kids
http://www.swissemb.org/kids

Index